Inside the Onion

Inside the Onion

Howard Nemerov

The University of Chicago Press
Chicago and London

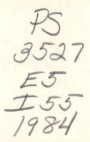
Howard Nemerov, a graduate of Harvard University in 1941, has taught at a number of colleges and universities and is now the Edward Mallinckrodt Distinguished University Professor of English at Washington University in St. Louis. He served as associate editor of *Furioso* magazine from 1946 to 1951 and was consultant in poetry to the Library of Congress from 1963 to 1964. Nemerov has won many notable literary awards, including the Levinson Prize from *Poetry* magazine, the Fellowship of the Academy of American Poets in 1971, the 1978 National Book Award, the 1978 Pulitzer Prize for Poetry, and the 1981 Bollingen Prize for poetry. He became a member of the National Institute of Arts and Letters in 1965 and of the American Academy of Arts and Letters in 1976. His published works include the following:

Verse: *The Image & the Law; Guide to the Ruins; The Salt Garden; Mirrors & Windows; New and Selected Poems; The Next Room of the Dream; The Blue Swallows; Gnomes & Occasions; The Western Approaches; The Collected Poems; Sentences; Inside the Onion*

Fiction: *The Melodramatists; Federigo, or the Power of Love; The Homecoming Game; A Commodity of Dreams & Other Stories; Stories, Fables & Other Diversions*

Nonfiction: *Poetry & Fiction: Essays; Journal of the Fictive Life; Reflections on Poetry & Poetics; Figures of Thought; Poets on Poetry* (editor)

The University of Chicago Press, Chicago 60637
The University of Chicago Press, Ltd., London

Library of Congress Cataloging in Publication Data

Nemerov, Howard.
Inside the onion.
  I. Title.
PS3527.E5L3   1984   811'.54   83-9312
ISBN 0-226-57244-7

For David, Alexander, Jeremy, with love

The author would like to thank the editors of the following journals for permission to reprint poems first appearing in their pages, some of them in earlier states and since revised.

Berkeley Poetry Review / *Bulletin of the Missouri Botanical Society* / *Bulletin of the St. Louis Art Museum* / *Harvard Magazine* / *Kenyon Review* / *Nebo* / *Ohio Journal* / *Paris Review* / *Perspective* / *Poetry, a Magazine of Verse* / *Quarter Moon* / *River Styx* / *The St. Louis Post Dispatch* / *Subject to Change* / *Threepenny Review* / *Untitled* / *Vanderbilt Poetry Review*

"Gnomic Variations for Kenneth Burke" was printed in an edition of forty copies by Louis D. Rubin, Jr., at the Tinker Press, Chapel Hill, and divided equally between author and printer for distribution to friends.

"The Air Force Museum at Dayton" was printed as one of a series of broadsides by Stuart Wright at the Palaemon Press Limited, Winston-Salem.

Contents

On His Own Terms

As with a liner at the speed of sound
Flying the sea, earth's weather left beneath,
All hurry is excluded from the hull
In streaming wind and night-shattering noise
And in the turbine blades that churn the cold
To fire and force trailing a ruin of smoke,

While inside, in low light, the master's moves
Are small and deliberate, their intervals
Quietly spaced as in recited rites
Traditionally prescribed by gravity
And far foresight; for certain that's the way
It is meant to be, one term of likening,
One term left out. So let it be that way.

Reading Pornography in Old Age

Unbridled licentiousness with no holds barred,
Immediate and mutual lust, satisfiable
In the heat, upon demand, aroused again
And satisfied again, lechery unlimited,

Till space runs out at the bottom of the page
And another pair of lovers, forever young,
Prepotent, endlessly receptive, renews
The daylong, nightlong, interminable grind.

How decent it is, and how unlike our lives
Where "fuck you" is a term of vengeful scorn
And the murmur of "sorry, partner" as often heard
As ever in mixed doubles or at bridge.

Though I suspect the stuff is written by
Elderly homosexuals manacled to their
Machines, it's mildly touching all the same,
A reminiscence of the life that was in Eden

Before the Fall, when we were beautiful
And shameless, and untouched by memory:
Before we were driven out to the laboring world
Of the money and the garbage and the kids

In which we read this nonsense and are moved
At all that was always lost for good, in which
We think about sex obsessively except
During the act, when our minds tend to wander.

In Memory of the Master Poet Robert Browning

Remembering that century and the one before
That seemed such inexhaustible springs of song,
Di quell'amor and *Dove sono* and the rest,
Orpheus wondering what he'd do without
Eurydice, the stuffed shirts in the stalls
Sobbing about Violetta, *croce e delizia*,
Coughing her love away, where did it go,
That wonderful stuff still with us now
But as a relic, the way they used to feel
Back then about Dreyfus, about Sedan,
La Gloire, Rhine Maidens with their swimming tits
Behind the scrim, now how could that have changed
And gone beyond our caring and our care?

When things are over that's what they are, over.
Master, I too feel chilly and grown old.
Like Ike said, he that conquered Europe, things
Are more like they are now than they ever were before.

To Alice out of Reach

This is chiefly to say, as Dryden did,
"Farewell, too little and too lately known,"
To a lady who as her husband wrote of her,
"Moved with the delicate balance of a sail."

I didn't know her well enough, but thought
Her fair and gentle, wise and kind and good,
Canonical adjectives all, they're all we have
For these occasions to which no one can rise
Nor ought to, maybe. I'd thoughtlessly thought
Our friendship had still many years to grow,
That there'd be time for silence and for speech
As for the music that in her generous house
Became a speaking silence more than speech,
And now there isn't time. Where the Bible says,
Chief refuge of an unobserving Jew
Affrighted of it early enough in life
So that he never did get over it,
There shall be no more time, I understand
The saying now not as it meant I should,
But as meaning that every death of every friend
Comes to the same, there shall be no more time.

Eternity may be too big a word
For any of us to take upon the tongue
(Sermons are silent twixt this line and next),
But that is what we have always in mind

When we say helplessly, caught in the social fact
That makes our truest feelings hypocrites,
Such standard things as "sorrow," "loss," "regret,"
And "Never again in this defaulting world, Alice,
Or our own waning lives, to see you more
Or hear your voice though saying nothing more
Remarkable or blessed than 'hello.'"

A Sprig of Dill

Small, fragrant, green, a stalk splits at the top
And rays out a hemisphere of twenty stems
That split in their turn and ray out twenty more
In hemispheres of twenty yellow stars
Targeted white, sprays mothered of spray
Displaying their tripled oneness all at once,
Radiant and delicate and loosely exact
As the cosmos in *The Comedy*, or as
The Copernican system on an orrery,
The quiet flowerworks of the mind of God
In an Age of Reason — that's in here. Out there,
The formless furnaces in Andromeda,
Hydra, The Veil, Orion's nightmare head.

Imprecated upon a Postal Clerk

Nor rain nor snow nor heat nor gloom of night
Can stay this surly civil servant safe
Behind the counter from imposing his
Confusion, slothful rudeness and delay
Upon the simplest procedures of exchange.

May he bring his children up on Grade-B milk,
Continue less intelligent than lint,
Bid thirteen spades in No-Trump out of greed,
And have real trouble finding his own ass
With both hands and a mirror and a torch.

Arthur

First year of graduate school he's in my class,
Bitter and bright and breakable as glass,
Stage-nigger talk, like going on all fours,
Intention and effect quite clear: *up yours*,

Till I the man his teacher "Arthur" saith
"Let's keep our consonants while we have our teeth."
He did, although it took him several years
To talk like whitey even in his beers.

Two days ago he passed me in his truck
He used for plastering, painting, and "You fuck,"
He yelled, "How do you do these fucking days?"
And he had every consonant in place.

Just yesterday they tell me a heart attack
Took him, his fifth white girl is left behind
With infant *numéro* n; in the last sack,
Arthur, who learned to mind; but never mind.

Striders

The little striders are so light and lean
They can walk atop the water's thinnest skin,
The surface tension that seals and varnishes
The table of the shallow-running stream
Supports their insubstantial shapes just as
In sunlight the sandy or stony floor beneath
Supports the quincunx of their abstract shadows,

But with the one and mortal difference that
Like mariners also committed to the deep
They cannot swim; putting a foot down wrong
Or hammered under in a heavy rain,
Caught in a breaking weather, they will drown.

At the Tomb of the Unknown Celebrity

You see how strange it is about the soul,
Hardly a one among the lot of us
Who witnessed his eccentric visit thought
Of him as anything other than he seemed,
Borne to us across an emptiness of space
And evanescing into it again
After the light went out, the lights went up,
Leaving us swept with empty empathy.

But now it turns out that he had a soul,
Or was one, dead in the middle of the way
Exactly, gone from the now here to the no where,
The undercover agent loved by us all
As by us all unknown, a stranger in
The unsuspected skin, his actor's art
Perfected to vanishing in the alien part.

Death of a Virgin

All during school we studied her. Life's joys
Are common to all men, but not the same
For each of us: maybe a thousand boys
Jerked themselves off while muttering her name.

Disseverings, Divorces

Disseverings, divorces, weddings that went
From woo to woe, from courtship through the courts
— imagine the army of them all arrayed
On some vast ground of neutral reckoning:
No judgment there, but merely memory and dismay
That each of them did love the other once.

The Difficulty of Doing Things Exactly Right

The Lord our God, who must do as He pleases,
Made me a Jew, the same as He did Jesus.
But now He's got a still more crucial question
Than why cross up a Jew to make a Christian:

Is He sorry to see that Equal Rights must mean
Hanging the Playmate of the Month between
Shoplifters? to see, with the Marquise de Sadie,
The pin-up girl become the Nail-up Lady?

Facing the Funerals

The bell, the book, the black and Roman candles,
The Buddha's smile, the jokes of Tao and Zen,
The wake, the dance, the solemn requiem mass,
The Resurrection and The Coming Forth by Day,
Wild grief and suttee and carnival's trespass —
The finding of a form of words to say
Men have their faiths as coffins have their handles,
Needed but once but handy to have then.

Total Immersion

for Jack Bridgman

How wounded Jesus' feelings would have been
Had humankind but said to Him with one
Though kindly voice of stone, "Now look here, son,
Don't do us any favors we don't want
Nor need nor haven't any use to have.
Just ask yourself first off who asked you to,
And none of that God in the manger stuff for us.
We're happy here, happier'n pigs in shit.

"You want to do us good, take death away
The way you said you come down here to do,
And we're all square. Forgiveness is so wonderful
We'd go on sinning till you couldn't not,
And only a suicide would then dare say
You done the sin against the Holy Ghost:
We'd see him in Hell before we let him go."

Poverty First Class, Poverty Tourist Class

There's holy poverty, elected by the prince,
By saviors for their disciples, by some saints,
Some crazies, some successful business types
Who being down opt out for down and out.

Then there's the other kind, that's forced, not chosen,
That's put upon a person not elect
And is a shame to him among his kin —
Though God knows why, seeing it's His ideal —

Who reads the whiskey ads, the girlie ads,
The colored ads for cruises to the sun
In winter, and may think what he may think
About his cold house in this pleasant land,

And should be shown the poster I've been shown
Of a lardy laughing man stood on a gold
Rolls Royce displaying a poster in his turn
That says in all simplicity "Poverty Sucks."

This My Modest Art

This my modest art is what I said
In early days, and now assert again
Against the age and its ever-affected
Apocalyptics, its fancy ladies and gents
Who see the World's end in so clear a light
That they regard high-minded suicide,
Pretended still if not accomplished yet,
As more than Dresden, Tokyo, and the rest,
So interested in ending they won't see
How much has ended, great cities knocked out,
High civilizations in their rubbled ruin,
Religions one thought stable finished in
Their own Jonestowns, the massacres of sects
Of women and children on a doctrinal point
By Christian militia and the lovely rest —

Maybe we kill only because we die,
And if we didn't die we might not kill;
But it's not what you'd bet real money on.

Last Things

Some thoughts you've doubtless thought as I have done
At twelve o'clock, or one: these others died,
How shouldn't I? It may be soon or late,
But is going to come, come (as they say) what may.

How will it be? the blue revolving light
Reflected on the rainy road one night,
The hospital, with the tubes stuck up your nose
And somebody else's blood patched into you?

There'll be a funeral service, sure there will,
To get you over with; your friends will say,
Your comfortable survivors dining out
On whatever time you've left them, comforting things,

Whatever they can think of or remember.
And you'll be over, you'll be done to a turn,
Whom they will think of at the oddest times:
How many pair of shoes ago was that?

Reverie of the Termite Queen

Sealed with my consort in the royal room
Under the hill that I have never seen
But made the makers of, I lie in state
While minions ply me with both food and drink

To cosset Majesty while I factor forth
The hundred million children whom I must
Outlive a hundred times before I may
Collapse the shrivelled whistle of my womb

At last effete and do what distinguished thing
One does to die. My proles, my infantry,
Parade on their endless errands hither and yon
Above my mystery, the soul of state,

Where I lie pulsing full with the ignorant host
That I dismiss into the world without,
Concerning which I am both dark and blind
As to what it may be, and why it is.

Calendars

At Christmas, for the New Year coming on,
The stores are colorful with calendars
To gift each other with, remembrances
Of time to come and to be followed through,

Appointments to be kept, accompanied
With moral maxims writ in ornate scripts,
With photographs of temples, flowers, tombs,
Endearing cats for those endearing cats endear;

Calendars thoughtful to companion us
With all conceits of Nature, Faith, and Art
Through all the seasons and the varied scenes
Where Time still begs his silent, sightless way.

You know the old story Ann Landers tells
About the housewife in her basement doing the wash?
She's wearing her nightie, and she thinks, "Well hell,
I might's well put this in as well," and then
Being dripped on by a leaky pipe puts on
Her son's football helmet; whereupon
The meter reader happens to walk through
And "Lady," he gravely says, "I sure hope your team wins."

A story many times told in many ways,
The set of random accidents redeemed
By one more accident, as though chaos
Were the order that was before creation came.
That is the way things happen in the world,
A joke, a disappointment satisfied,
As we walk through doing our daily round,
Reading the meter, making things add up.

The fountain's silver pulse
Falls in a filthy pool.

— what a filthy male
Chauvinist remark!

But all I said was just
The fountain's silver pulse
Falls in a filthy pool
Go out to Lewis Park
And see it any time you like.

— Lues Park? I knew it!
You just keep out of my Lues Park.

That must be what they call
A homonymph. But still. . .

The arithmetic teacher used to say
Put it in terms of money
The kids will understand it.

The old black cook at camp
Said sprinkle sugar on shit
And the boys will eat it.

And it's said about The Bard
Himself that a dirty mind
Is a perennial resource.

The fountain's silver pulse
Falls in a filthy pool.

Assembly Line, Fighter Factory

It's seven stages down the line
To follow out the full design
Where each successive plane presents
The harmony of its elements
More integrated than the last,
Guns, engines, wiring, wings made fast;
As in a time-lapse study of
A creature that's conceived in love,
Perfecting daily from the germ
The wished-for end, the final form.

Tributaries of long thought
Make up the current toward the taut
Machines that wait high fin by fin
Out at the finish of the line,
The armed and armored painted ships
Made ready for their destined trips
To the customers Germany, Japan,
Greece, Turkey, Israel, Iran,
The consummation of their strength
In blood and dust and death at length.

Prayer of the Middle Class at Ease in Zion

Dear god, dear goddess, how you tease us on
About the seasons and around the clock,
Bemuse us with the same conceits, deceits,
That we're considered deathless while we're here

Who after will be done with and be gone
As no one has been done and gone before,
Not sultans, empresses, magnificoes
Of every wealth and all the quality

Along with proles and stupes of every sort
Compeers at last where it no longer counts,
Nigger and Whitey equalized at last
In the long run, and how long a run it is —

Dear god, dear goddess, whether you exist
Or fail to exist, be not a trouble to us
Now in October when the cicadae climb
To the highest branches and sing themselves to death.

Wintering

A prism hung in a window to the south
Spangles the room, the kitchen, the hall beyond,
With rainbows from the time of Orion's rise
Until the sun climbs up so high in May
His angle gets too thin to manage anything
More than a splinter of spectrum on the floor
Beneath the sill; but who needs rainbows then,
With the sun his radiant self all summer long?

No diamond from deep earth could celebrate
So well our long engagement with the world
As faceted glass dangled against the pane
To swing advantage from the sun's long swing
Low through the darkness and the burning cold
Until, sweet chariot, he brings us up
Again, poking the crocus through the snow
Again, and once more turns might into may.

Having a Mind to Change the World

Twice a year and during Sunday sleep
The Republic finds itself unanimously
Agreed except for Indianapolis
To shift the sun through fifteen degrees of arc
In a trice or two by twiddling some knobs,
Whereon the sun obedient moves back and forth
At the mere commandment of Democracy.

Not Joshua in the Vale of Ajalon
Did more than stay the sun a space, while we
By will alone twitch him about the sky,
Taking a daylight hour from the dawn
And giving it to evening, even if
We Indian-givers later take it back.
What shall be denied unto this people
That with a thought thus moves both heaven and earth?

Learning

Two-petalled, blue, with yellow stamens, this
Shy fellow halfway folded in his leaf
Grows almost furtively from the side of the stem
Whose top is occupied by two leaves opposite.

Small armies of him growing everywhere,
And yet his name not writ in any book
That I can find, so I have christened him
Nemerovia vulgaris, or Common Piss-Winkle.

Some people will do almost anything
To go down in history, get their names in the book.

Marvell

Slow, dear Marvell? Vegetables are slow?
Your mistress may be, empires surely are,
Even love, given a millennial Reich to grow.

But here it isn't August yet, and yet
The painted gourd's already gone over the wall,
The grapevine's wrestling with the tops of trees,

Moss roses are firing a steady bloom a day,
Two castor beans darken the picture window,
Sunflowers are up to toppling at twelve feet tall —

Good god, dear man, consider Jonah's gourd
And be amazed thereat, and at the speed
Of grass and hay and all green growing things.

Belli

for Miller Williams

Like many another atheist reading the Bible
His whole life long, the keystone of the arch
Holding the rest in place with endless trouble,
Loving the god and jeering at the church,

He saw the odds as clear as Dante did
But funnier, had the refusal of heaven's plenty,
The blood and gristle of the paschal kid,
Per la contradizione che nol consente.

Rome was Jerusalem, was Nazareth,
And ordinary as heaven to his wit
That would not tell the sinner from the sin,

That made the Christ live here, deep in the shit
With the rest of us, and not to be found dead
In the Vatican if that is they'd let Him in.

To Kay Boyle

Now listen, Mother B, somebody said
You'd decided it was time for you to die
And you were going abroad to see your kids,
Those odd grey persons, one last time.

I won't stand still for that, I don't believe it.
Continuez, my dear, *continuez*,
That old instruction from the atelier
Still goes, but don't you go.

Hang in there, Mother B, a girl like you
Should set a better example. Tell you what,
If you don't show up at my funeral
Then I won't go to yours. So there.

A Moon Eclipsed

"You see," the learned astronomer said to us,
"When instruments were born into the world,
Map, globe and chart, astrolabe and orrery,
And after them the planetarium
Projecting the stars as from inside the eyes,
They brought along out of the earlier earth
A grand consortium of remaindered gods
With their associated nymphs and satyrs,
Centaurs and giants, which only slowly faded;
But when that chimaeric thereomorphic chorus
Ceased from their song and presently disappeared,
The telescopes would work as well, the maps
Still better, if not adorned with giant forms,
And we were left alone with nameless mind
Projecting its immense geometries
At the speed of light, the limiting speed of time,
To the end of our more perfect understanding."

So when we stayed up all that night to see
(but was it seeing, or seeing's opposite?)
A second darkness move across the night,
We saw exactly what he said we should:
The transit of the Earth with Sun and Moon
Casting a shadow intercepted and cupped
(a small vanilla scoop in a cone of dark)
As of a golf ball sitting on a tee
So big as to conceal it from the ground

Till it fell off the other side and life
Continued on its ordinary course
As it had always done. We saw it with
Our stereoscopic, single-power eyes.

A Grain of Salt

Swords into ploughshares, what a simple thing
Isaiah wished for, when compared to this
Stunning free offer from a pair of king-
doms come to trade their nukes in on a kiss

And chicken on the world's great suicide pact,
Agreed by treaty that on the deciding day
Conjoined in one big hard-to-follow act
Both tribes will throw their boomerangs away.

Gnomic Variations for Kenneth Burke

*An answer can seem wholly radiant only with those for whom
the question itself has radiance.*

A Rhetoric of Motives

I

The only reason I'd care to be a king
Would be to hear the subjects speak their mind
And know that meant their minds belonged to me:
"The King's English" — imagine, owning a language!

II

The senses and the mind deceive each other,
So Pascal said, maybe remembering
The terse debate Democritus overheard
Between the two, mind claiming loftily
That sweet is by convention, cold likewise
Is by convention, while in reality
Nothing exists but atoms and the void;
To which the senses rise indignant crying
"Miserable mind! it is from us you take
The evidence with which you would destroy us;
Your victory will be your own downfall."

III

"Whatever the nonverbal, there are words for it."
K.B., "Variations on the Word 'Providence'"

The Tao, the echoing spaces of a fugue,
The Cloud of Unknowing, The Clear Light of the Void,
Nothing to see but blind light to see it by;

36

Or else Nature going it on her own,
Blind mouths arranged in a fast food chain
With fucking to bridge the generation gap.

IV
When I first read Forster's famous battle cry
Only Connect, prefaced to *Howards End* —
Title designed as if to make me think
— I thought he'd meant to say "Only
Connecticut," but was interrupted by
A person on business from Cos Cob, because
The rebus represents Connect and Cut
Wedded and kept apart by Ego the I —
All dialectic in its nutmeg state.

V
My own small contribution to the great
Debate between the body and the soul
As to which should rule alone, is only this:
The lewdest image I was ever shown,
The filthiest suggestive pornographic piece,
Turned out to be an aerial photograph
Of sand dunes in sunshine and deep shadow.

VI
Between the senses five and Beldame Kind
Lies language, our fluid coupling with the world —

Incomprehensible, I hope you understand,
Because I said it plainly as I could.

We pause for these commercial messages:
"Man is the Cadillac of animals."
"The body is the Chris-Craft of the soul."
"The image on our new Phenomenal TV
Is so absolutely definite and clear
We can't even show it to you on your screen,
Which doesn't have the resolution, doesn't have
The definition, to do justice to
Its revelation of the empty eye."

VII

We have pursued the furious course of the world
As it ran from "If only . . ." to "If and only if . . . ,"
Kept faith with the author's egomaniac trade,
And followed the bedtime story of the world
Which may indeed have end, although so far
The children fall asleep before the end.

Kenneth, as you told me a time ago
How "We who used to elbow each other aside
Are closing ranks," now the fury of knowledge fades
And dialectic, if it do remain,
Remains the shell-game of its former self,
Unbeatable and obvious as language

Whose Gödelian and Delphic word has ever been
Don't look under the hood while driving the car —
May it be our hope appropriate to grow
Into the next phase as into the former ones,
And go upstairs about as often as down,
And to as many times a day as fro.

This Present Past

The tulip's cup falls open helplessly,
The redbud's petals are already dust,
The trees are dropping all their various dreck
Pertaining to generation; once again
The spring has gone, as we complain it does
Year after year, before we had the time
To take it in.
                    But brief as flowering
Has always been, our power to attend
Is briefer by far, and intermittent, too.
We look at the iris, say how beautiful,
And look no more, nor watch the fail and fall
Of its bruised flags. So runs the world away,
As blown about upon the rainy wind
The keys of the maple's kingdom copter down.

Graffiti

Tend to the underground, the underworld,
The infrastructure of the genitals
And the rectum's subterranean rectitudes,
The reigning bladder and bowel's imperium,
Necessity's facilities far from home,

Wherever the body lords it all alone
And makes filthy remarks about the soul,
That soiled aristocrat caught out, caught short ·
With its pants down and its bare face hanging out
In a neighborhood not safe to be at night,

Where the writing on the wall writes of itself,
Where LADIES and GENTS become revolting signs,
And every saying is a compressed cry
For the last things of love, and the wet white tiles
Exchange the mournful messages of the gay.

A Blind Man at the Museum

His wife is pushing a pram with twins before them,
He keeps in touch with a hand against her back,
And going sightless along the galleries
Listens to her mild voice describing things
While the speechless twins, like seeing eyes, look up.

They walk past windows giving on the past
Of grazing cows and crucifixions and
Self-portraits where the painter's mirrored eyes
Reflect themselves unseeing in the plane
Eternity of art, unable to look out.

A strangeness, just. But I imagined him
As having been, before he lost his sight,
Himself a painter, or if not that a great
Authority who has in his head by heart
Much that she reads the names, dates, titles of

To the twins who see but cannot know or say
The scumble of the black impasto'd skull
Behind all this, the agony of the eye
That sees the hand that acts but cannot see
Beneath the finish of the age, the art.

She sees, and says, they slowly push along
Between the walls, his hand against her back,
The seeing eyes, like pilot-fish, roll on,
A dumbshow of predicaments untold
Moving familiarly among the worlds.

Graven Images

for Jean Tucker

So many lightstruck likenesses there are,
Passport and portrait, postcard, even Art;
The news, the faces in the news, the ads
Inventing envy, there must be a great many
More than the number of persons now alive,
And maybe more than all that ever were —

Such stillness from such evanescence snapped
And shuddered by a falling guillotine
Across a glass —
                  The subjects taken thus,
To empty eternity exposed, have been
Developed by emulsions and by salts,
Printed in mummified facsimiles
And fixed by drying liquids in the dark-
rooms where their faithless ikons come to light:
The frozen sections through a living face,
The candid shots that paralyze the sea.

Lucretian Shadows

Suave, mari magno turbantibus aequora ventis, etc.

De Rerum Natura

1.

It's nice, when the wind blows the waves up high as hills,
To stand on shore and watch the ship go down
All hands aboard. Not that we wish bad luck
To any soul on earth; but it relieves
Our daily anxieties to see disaster hit
As long as it hits the neighbors and not us.

It's why we read the papers, watch the news.

2.

Lying in bed, watching the morning news,
I saw how a cameraman by his good luck
Had got himself set up in the liner's bows
Just after she had hit a fishing boat
Which split and drew down under after it
A couple of fishermen in yellow slickers
Drowning as easy as falling off a log
And at light speed transmitted to the world.

The cold and tilting sea, blue black and green
With ornament of lacy silver spray,
The little yellow slickers sudden as dream

Appearing in the iris'd lens and then
Sudden as waking gone, the world and I
Snug as a bug in a rug and warm as a worm,
Warm as a worm in the compost heap in winter —

That's how things happen, they say. That's how it is.

Fish Swimming amid Falling Flowers

*comme le pan de mur jaune que peignit avec tant de science et
de raffinement un artiste à jamais inconnu, à peine identifié. . .*

On a ground of pale gold water of watered silk
The painter of a thousand years ago
Angled his wrist so rapidly and right
The hairs of the brush bent in obedience
To do the swerve and diagonal of these fish
Swimming in space, in water, on watered silk,
And stippled in the detail of their scales,
The pale translucency of tail and fin,
And dotted at the brush's very tip
The falling petals and the petals fallen,
And scattered a few lotus and lily pads
Across the surface of the watered silk
Whose weave obedient took all this in,
The surface petal-flat, the fish beneath
The golden water of the watered silk,

So that a thousand years of the world away
On this millennially distant shore of time
The visitor to the museum may stare
Bemused down through the glass hermetic seal
At the silken scroll still only half unrolled
Past centuries invisible as air
To where the timeless, ageless fish still swim,
And read the typescript on the card beside
That says "Fish Swimming Amid Falling Flowers"
A thousand years ago, and seeing agree
That carp did always swim, and always will,

In just that way, with just that lightning sweep
Of eye, wrist, brush across the yielding silk
Stretched tight with surface tension as the pool
Of pale gold water, pale gold watered silk.

Adam and Eve in Later Life

On getting out of bed the one says, "Ouch!"
The other "What?" and when the one says "I said
'Ouch,'" the other says "All right, you needn't shout."

Deucalion and Pyrrha, Darby and Joan, Philemon and
    Baucis,
Tracy and Hepburn — if this can happen to Hepburn
No one is safe — all rolled up into two,
Contented with the cottage and the cottage cheese
And envied only by ambitious gods . . .

Later, over coffee, they compare the backs of their hands
And conclude they are slowly being turned into lizards.
But nothing much surprises them these days.

Morality

All during dinner he nearly lost himself,
Whenever she leaned forward, looking down
The deep Vee of her loose unbuttoned shirt.
If anything could make him think, that would,
And to such effect that later on that night,
Having looked her down, he decided to look her up.

There was no phone book in the motel room.
So he got her from the Gideon instead:
Her number was PRoverbs 5 3456,
Extension 727. So that was that.

But later, as he laid him down to sleep,
He thought how all good children go to heaven,
While as for all the other children, well,
Strange woman . . . and wondered would he ever cease
To wonder at the consternation could be caused
In a perfect stranger by a couple of bumps in a blouse.

Inside the Onion

Slicing the sphere in planes you map inside
The secret sections filled up with the forms
That gave us mind, free-hand asymmetries
Perfecting for us the beautiful inexact

That mathematic may approximate
And clue us into but may never mate
Exactly: bulb, root, fruit of the fortunate fall
That feeds us with the weeps and utter tang

Of the ovoid circles and the slipshod squares,
Triangles rounded at their corners, space
Geometrized resisting its geometry
Imperfectly, as it was meant to do —

Like stepping on a raft and rocking it
So that its ripples square the corners off
For just a second before the Mad Housewife
Soothes down the angles and bends them into curves

As worrying her secret might be known
And ours, empiric and its theory
Be one again, her crispen crystalline
Arithmetic raveled and riddled in Time,

Her rounding off and averaging out
That favors the evenses against the odds
And makes the onion, holding in our tears,
One and the same throughout the in and out.

Acts of God

Are exhibitions of bad taste on a scale
Beyond belief, filling your living room
With mud or lava, blowing the schoolhouse roof
Down on the parking lot, tossing the boats
Out of the marina and smashing them across
The highway's back, piquantly fixing for
The earthquake to catch his people on their knees
Good Friday morning; if Attila the Hun
Had done the hundredth part of what God does
You wouldn't ask him to dinner at your house.
But God gets away with it time and time again
And gets adored for doing it as well
As lest he do it to us another time.
The hope is our prayers will make Him nicer, but
It don't look likely, and to make it worse
An Act of God is anything at all
That lets the insurance people off the hook.

The Air Force Museum at Dayton

Under the barrel roof in solemn gloom
The weapons, instruments, and winged shapes,
The pictured dead in period costumes,
Illustrate as in summary time-lapse

Photography the planetary race
That in the span of old men still around
Arose from Kitty Hawk to sky to space,
Cooped up as if it never left the ground.

After the pterodactyl and the Wright
Brothers every kite carries a gun
As it was meant to do, for right and might
Are properly understood by everyone.

Destructive powers, and speeds still unforeseen
But half a life ago, stand passive here,
Contraptions that have landed on the Moon
Or cancelled cities in a single flare.

When anything's over, it turns into art,
Religion, history; what's come to pass
Bows down the mind and presses upon the heart:
The ancient bombsight here enshrined in glass

Is the relic left us of a robot saint
With a passion for accuracy, who long ago
Saw towns as targets miniature and quaint,
Townsfolk invisible that far below.

She

So Dante exalted his Beatrice, a girl
"Of great beauty and utterly without charm"
Of whom his wife once wrote Ann Landers, Ann
My husband is a decent kindly man
Though on the road a lot, but has this thing
About a dame's been dead for half his life
He's writing this enormous poem about
And I want to know should I bring the matter up?
The wise woman answered Better leave it lay,
And added Gemma baby you need help.

So whether you call your girl O goddess or
You stupid cunt is some damn thing to do
With your psychology or how you feel
Or what she is or some other bloody thing
Nobody understands or ever will.
She is a point of faith, a mystery, and
Like God the Just she has a secret name
Distinguishable only to initiates
Muttering betsy clara jenny jane
In bed and childbed and the holy grave.

Epiphany

Brief as it was, the season of good will
Is gone. So farewell for another year
To Yggdrasil and the homely Northern Lights
Strung out till Twelfth Night on the evergreen
And axial tree that till we dismantled it
Went on pulsing its spectral sequences
Amber and blue and red and green in patterns
Like signals from a distant system not
Regarded, not interpreted, as if
Meaning to say some random-seeming thing
Wanted deciphering till the code came clear,
The unique product of some pair of primes
That would allow us to square the whole thing off
And translate its points and intervals:
"O yes, we read you. We have Christmas too.
He died for us, we kill for Him. Like you."

For ———, to Protect Her from Burns

You know, my dear, had we been born
    Three hundred years apart
The neither of us would have bothered the other,
    We wouldna' ha' gi'en a fart.

But thirty year's the difference, dear,
    And thirty year apart's
What we have got between us now
    Though not between our hearts.

It's stupid Mother Nature, dear,
    It's mocking old Dame Kind
That keeps the body growing old
    Without she keeps the mind.

Old age with youth will hardly sort,
    Though it's a dirty trick
Old age it is, where everything
    Gets harder but the prick.

Religionists

If we can't love, believe, and fear their God
(all three at once), they still demand we should
Be humbly respectful of their faith, and of them
For faithing it when it is avowedly
Absurd, impossible, and unbelievable.

If even that's beyond us, and we're lost
For good, the sorry least we can do, they think,
Is show a proper reverence for their reverence.

A Dog's Life

I

Here now's another dog has died, three weeks ago.

— We shouldn't have another, we're too old.

— Agreed, unless one creeps up to the door
Too young to walk, the way the last one was,
And we take it in.
                  — It takes us in again
Is what you mean. Your animals are like
Reviewers, you outlive the lineage of them,
There'll be one left to howl above your grave.

— It's love, the Guest says, makes the world go 'round.

— Love, says the Host, that moves the sun and stars,
Where physics is philosophy and faith as well.

II

So here she is, a mere three weeks too late,
Picked up in traffic and with no dog-tags,
Collar and flea-collar both too tight,
A little pewter-colored curly pup
With a remarkable grin, who cuddles up
Between us nights and modifies the marriage,
And dances up and down on her hind feet

Before a tabled jury of dour cats
Who take three days before they take her in.

Her name, or so the household poet says,
Is evidently Wool Ball, Wool for short.

III

The last one took a week or more to name,
Sniffen was too Dickensian, but then
Snifkin was Dostoyevskian and right
For a hound with bloodshot red-rimmed eyes
As if some other party lived in him
And now and then looked out. He died, or they did,
Of some dripping disorder of the blood
That neither we nor the vet ever understood.

And now here's Wool Ball, shortly Wool for short,
That we belong to as she belongs to us
—a funny word, *belong*, be, longing, long.—

And here goes immortality again,
Old age, another dog, this one more time.

First Light

Only for wanting to see the world made new
In every weather, growing its colors again
Out of the brown, grey, black, the muted flowers
In Lennahan's garden beginning to burn orange
And lavender and blue, the steady sequencing
Of green and yellow and red, green arrow,
Green yellow red again above the road,
With ritual precision and gravity
Asserting The City in its formal law
More powerful and pure for emptiness
Than in the later traffic of the day,
I walk out of darkness and into first light,
Patrol and precinct of the speechless ghosts:
An early worker, a late-returning drunk,
Four lonesome joggers slowly fleeing Death,
The Harvester delivering The Globe.

Notes

At the Tomb of the Unknown Celebrity
 Michael Patrick Bilon, who played E. T. in the movie.

Belli
 Giuseppe Gioacchino Belli, 1791–1863, known to the people of
Rome as their poet. A selection from his more than two thousand
sonnets has been translated by Miller Williams and published by
Louisiana State University Press: *Sonnets of Giuseppe Belli* (Baton
Rouge, 1981). The translator has also provided an introduction to
the volume. More about Belli's life and work may be found in
that introduction, as well as in Eleanor Clark, *Rome and a Villa*,
expanded edition (New York: Atheneum, 1982).

Fish Swimming amid Falling Flowers
 The picture, in the St. Louis Art Museum, is attributed to the
northern Sung painter Liu Ts'ai. Proust's painter of the *pan de
mur jaune* is, of course, Vermeer. Readers interested to check out
Liu Ts'ai's vision against current carp going about their business
will do well to look down from the bridge over the lake at the
Japanese garden called Sei-wa En at Shaw's Garden in St. Louis.
Between life and art there are differences, but only the ones you
would expect; ink is thicker than water, not by much.